Make a Salad

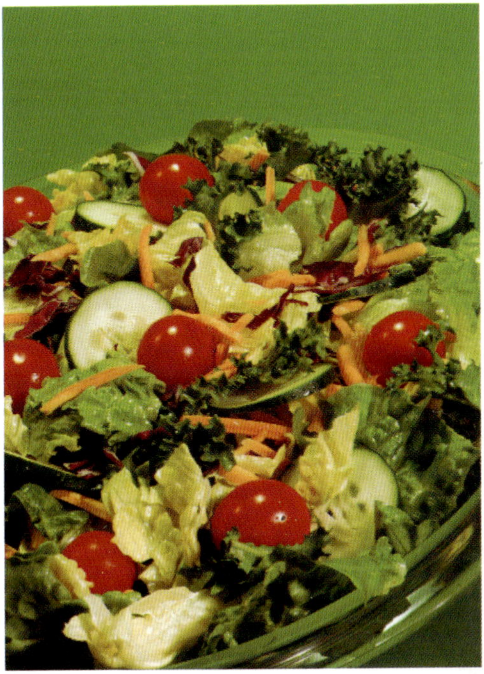

written by Pam Holden

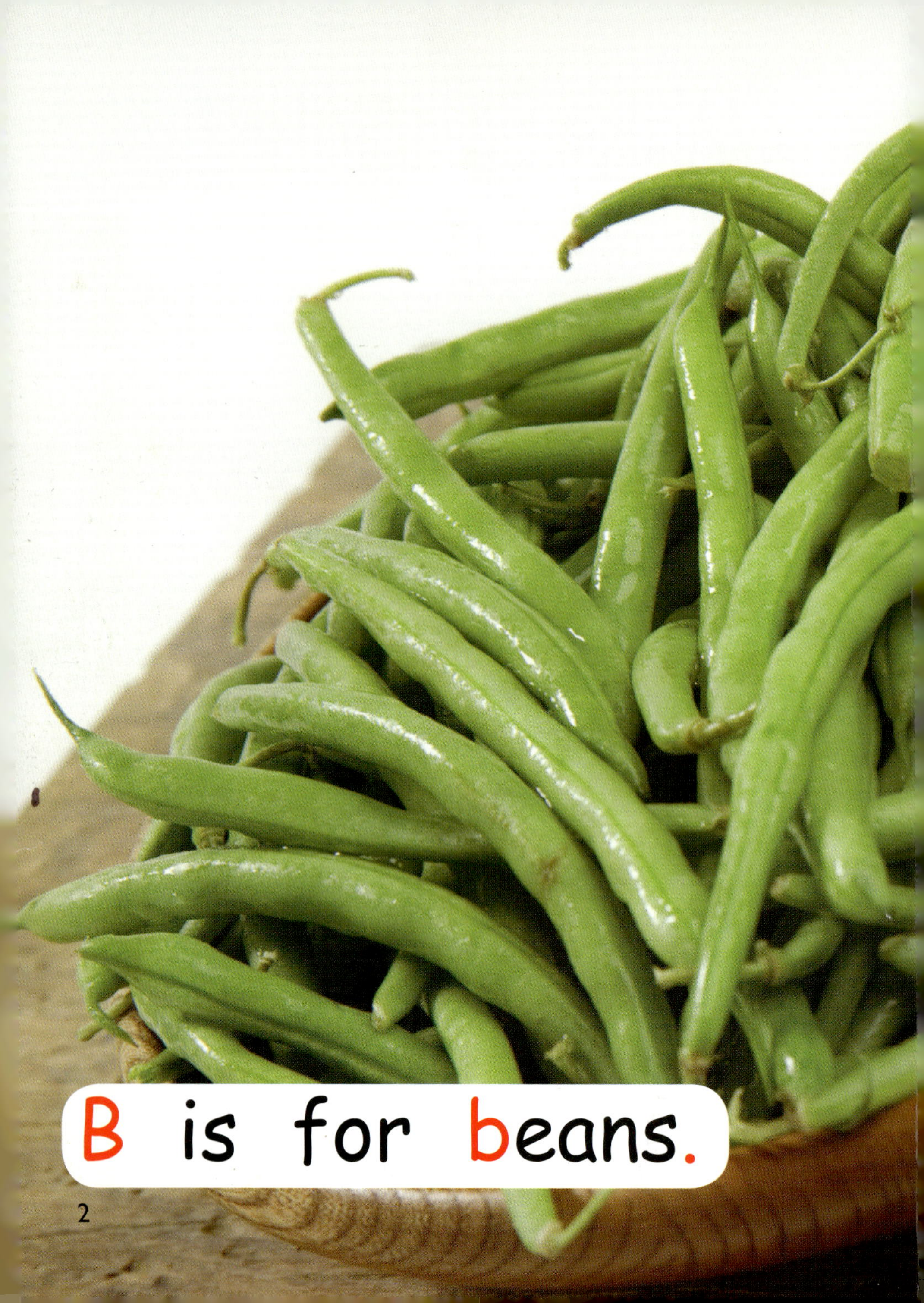

B is for beans.

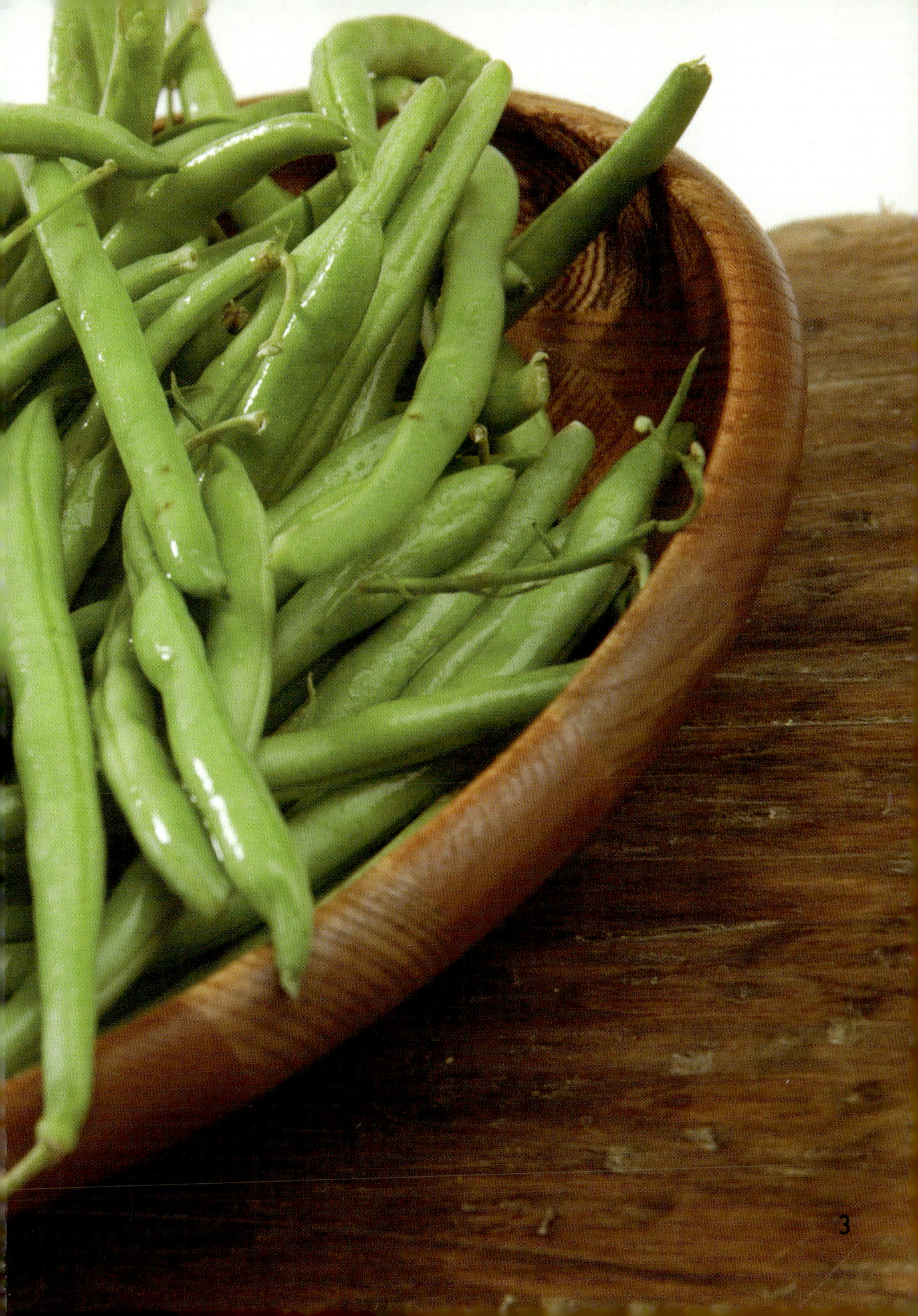

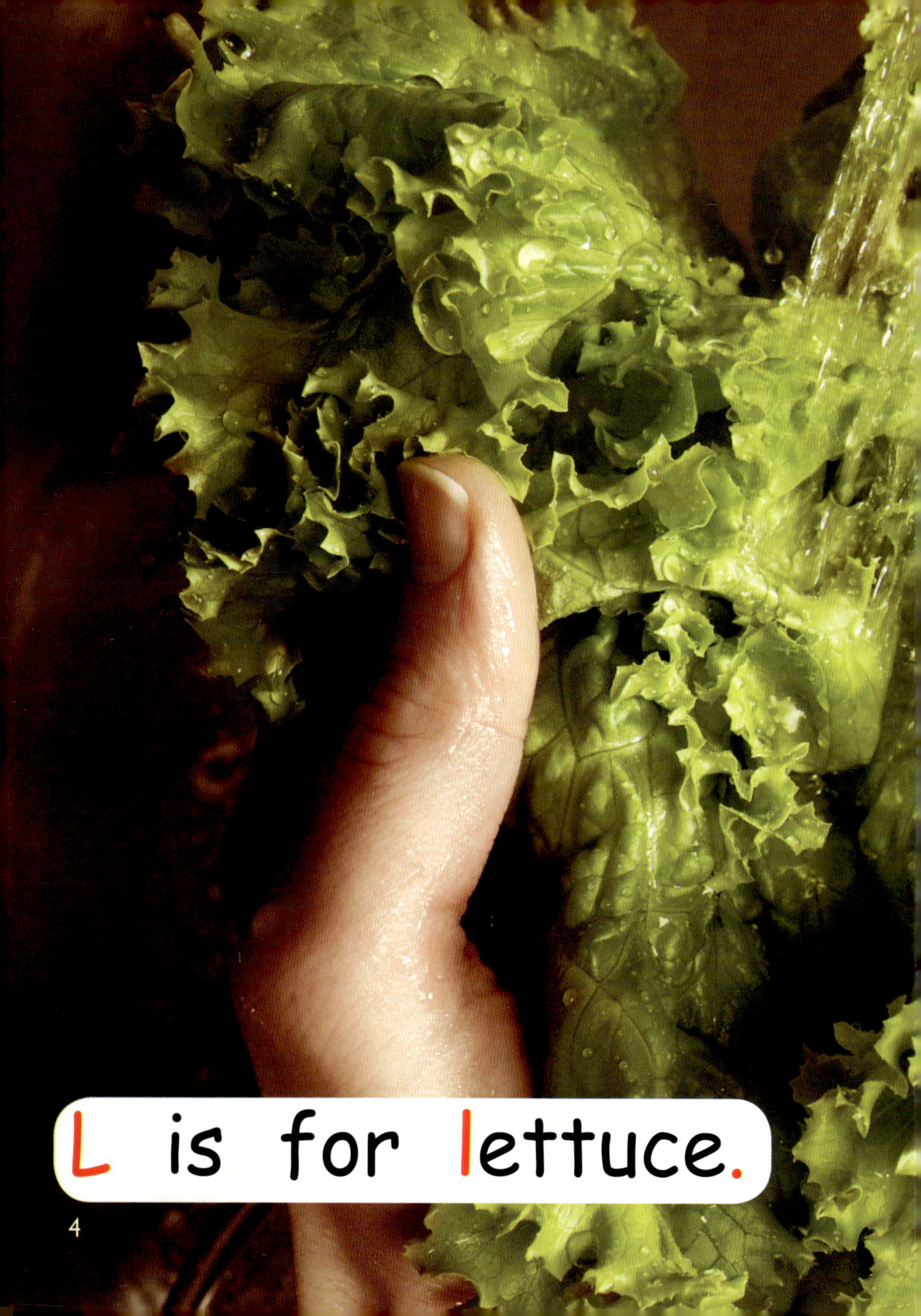

L is for lettuce.

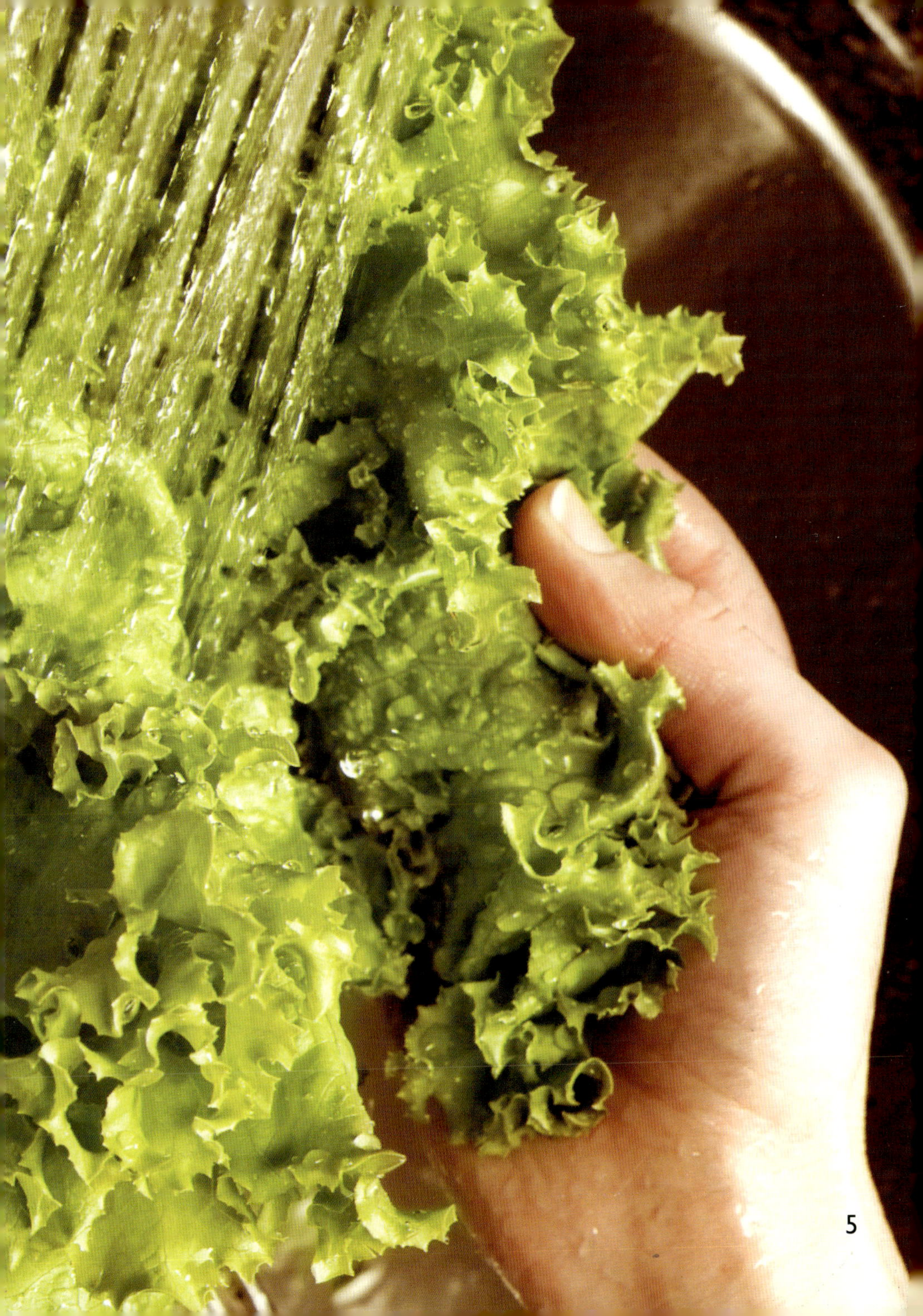

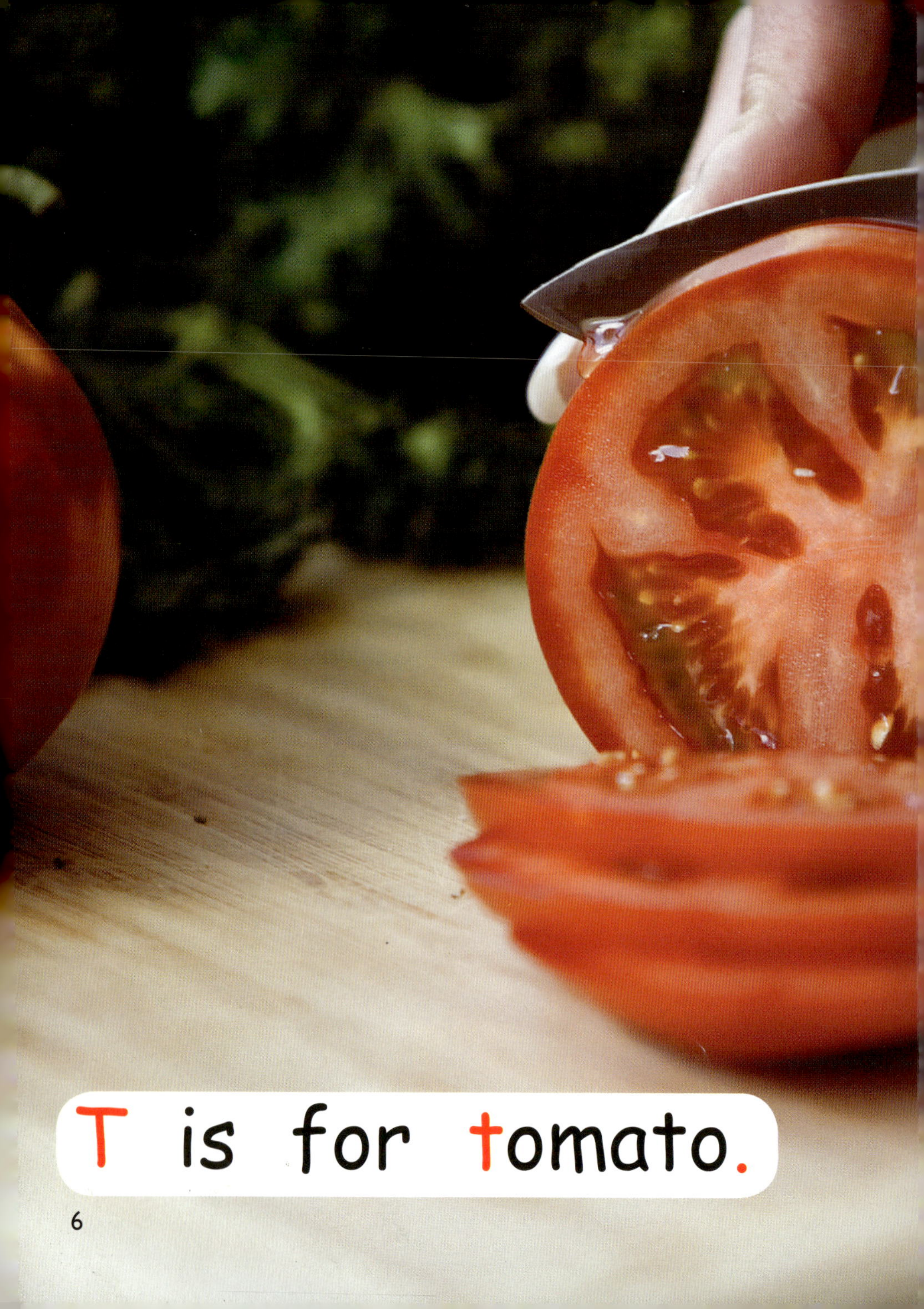

T is for tomato.

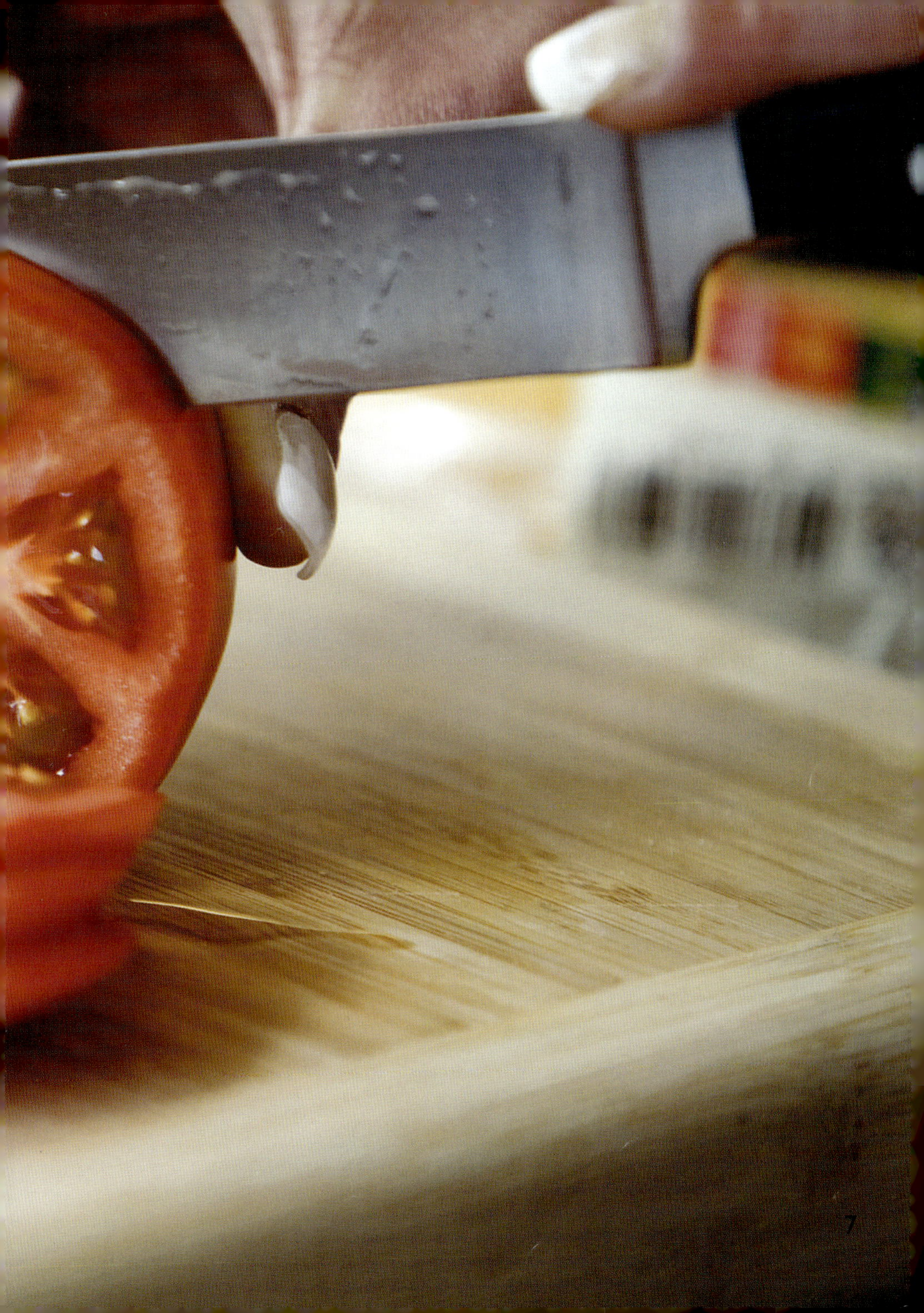

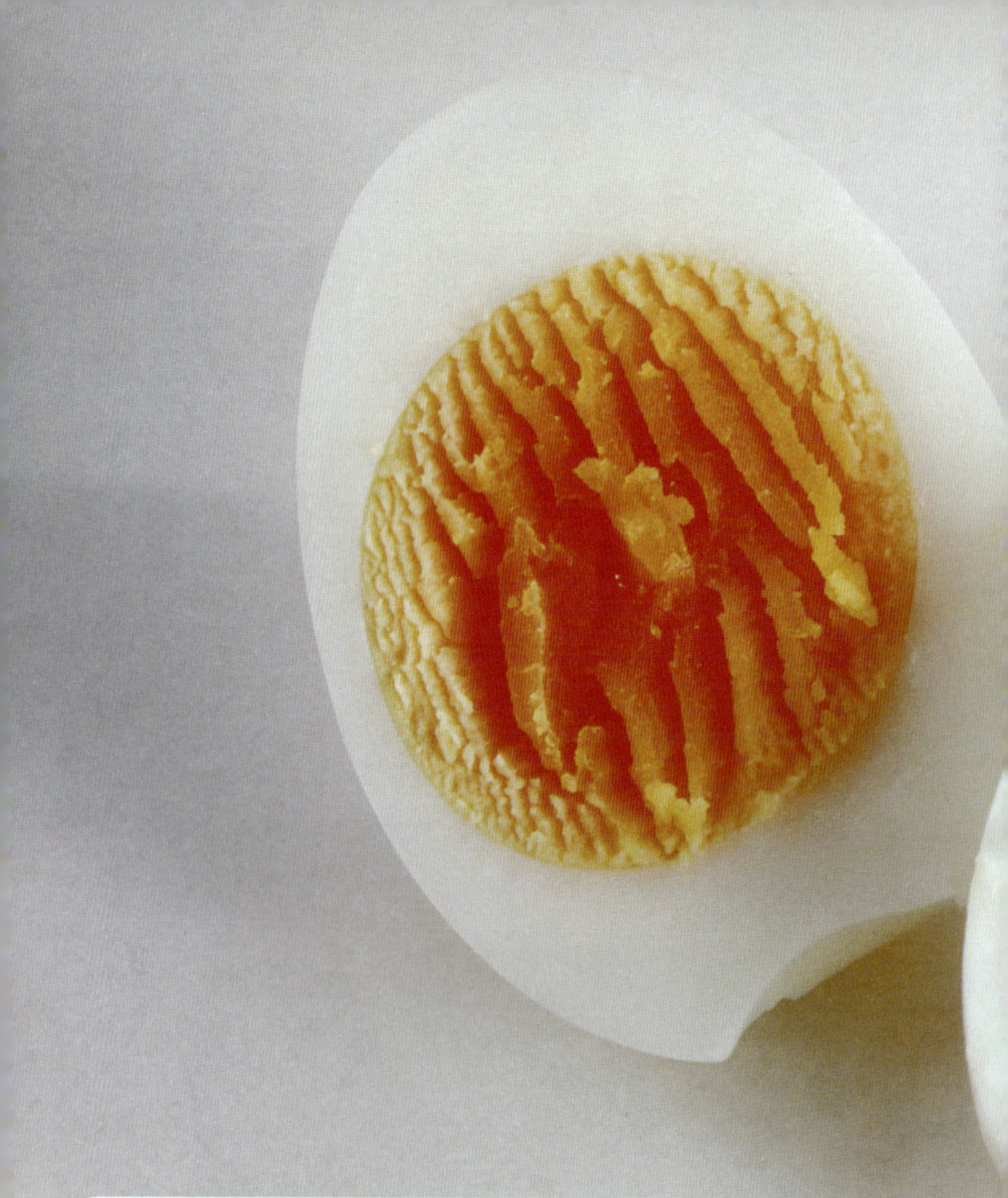

E is for egg.

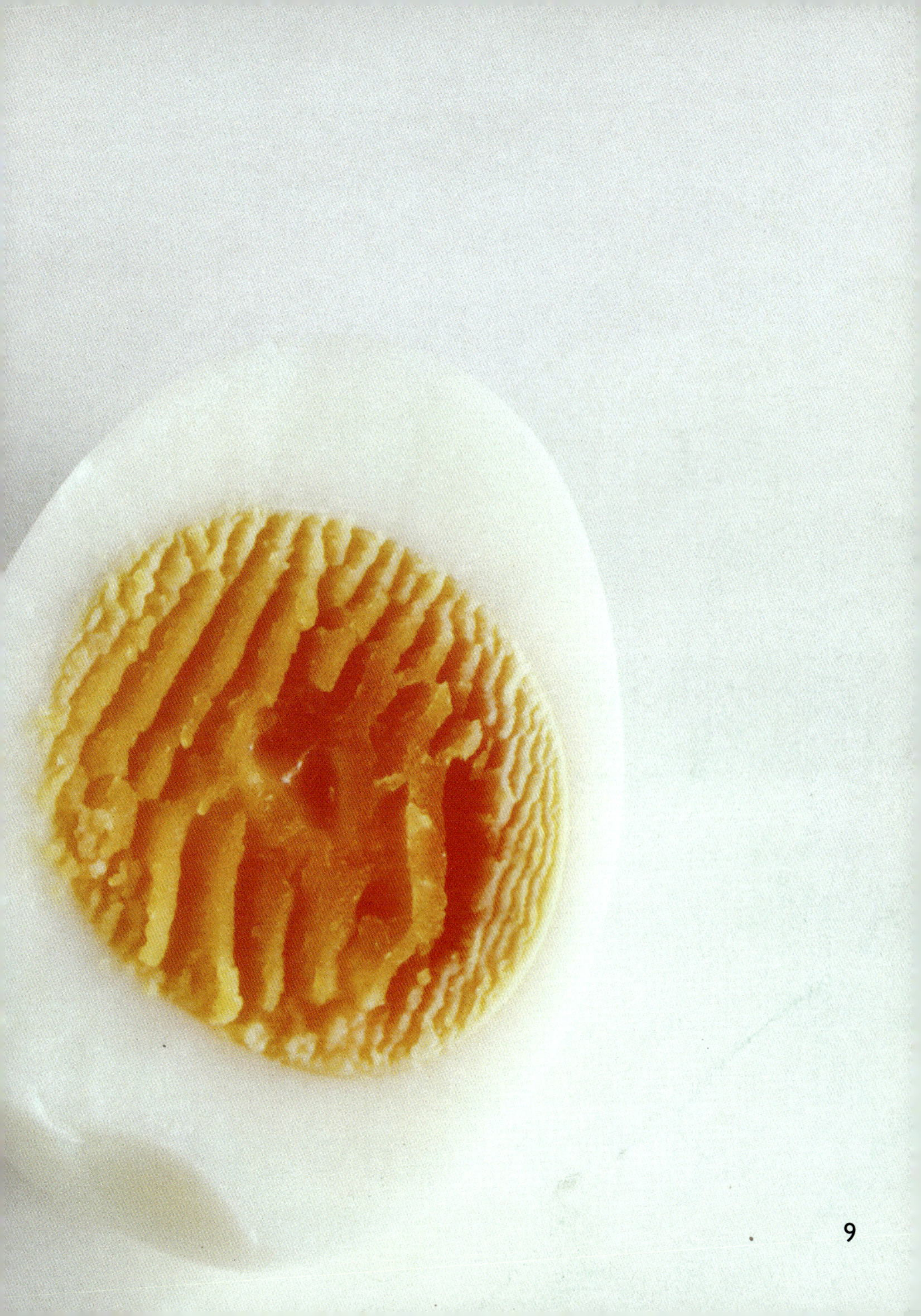

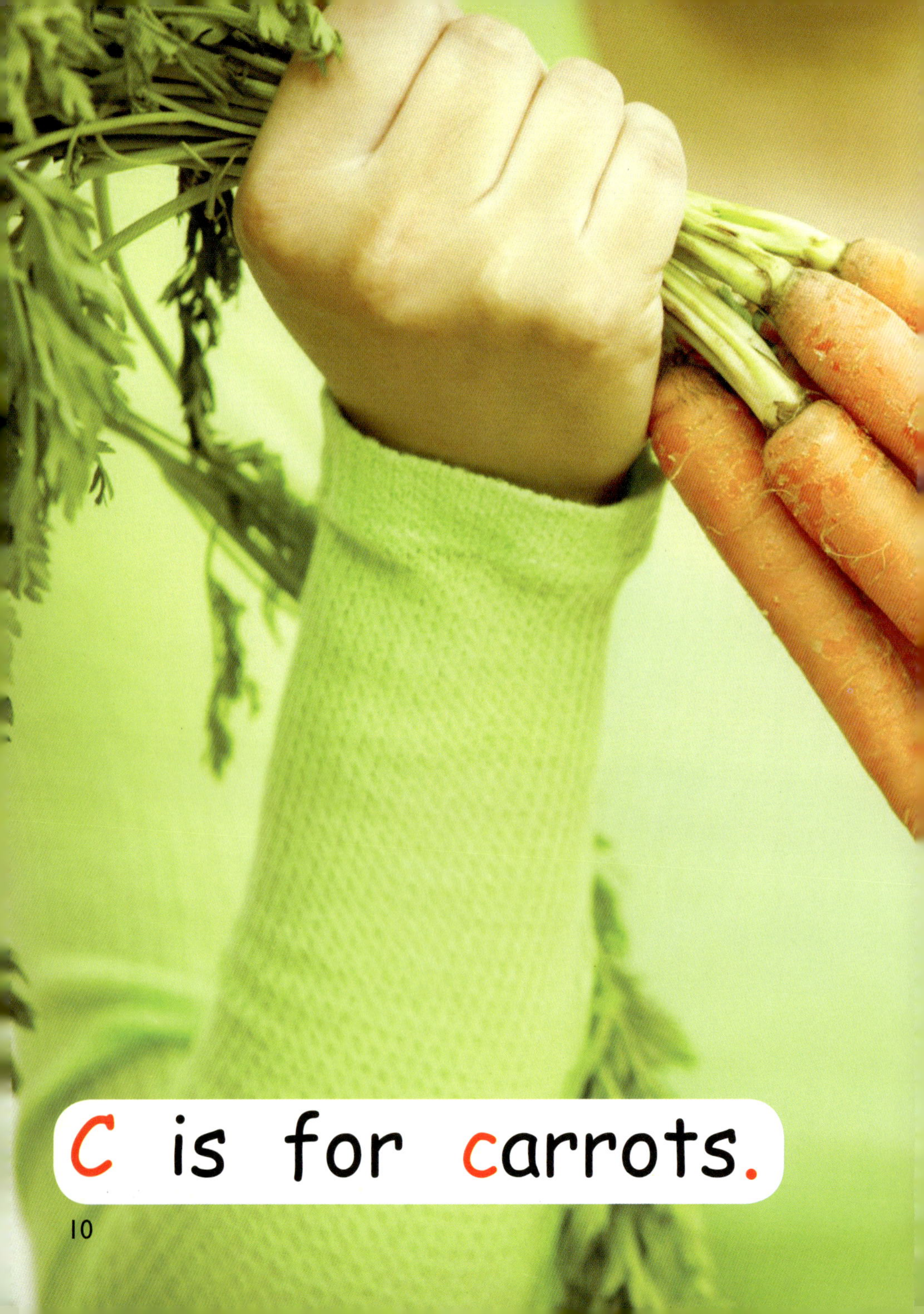

C is for carrots.

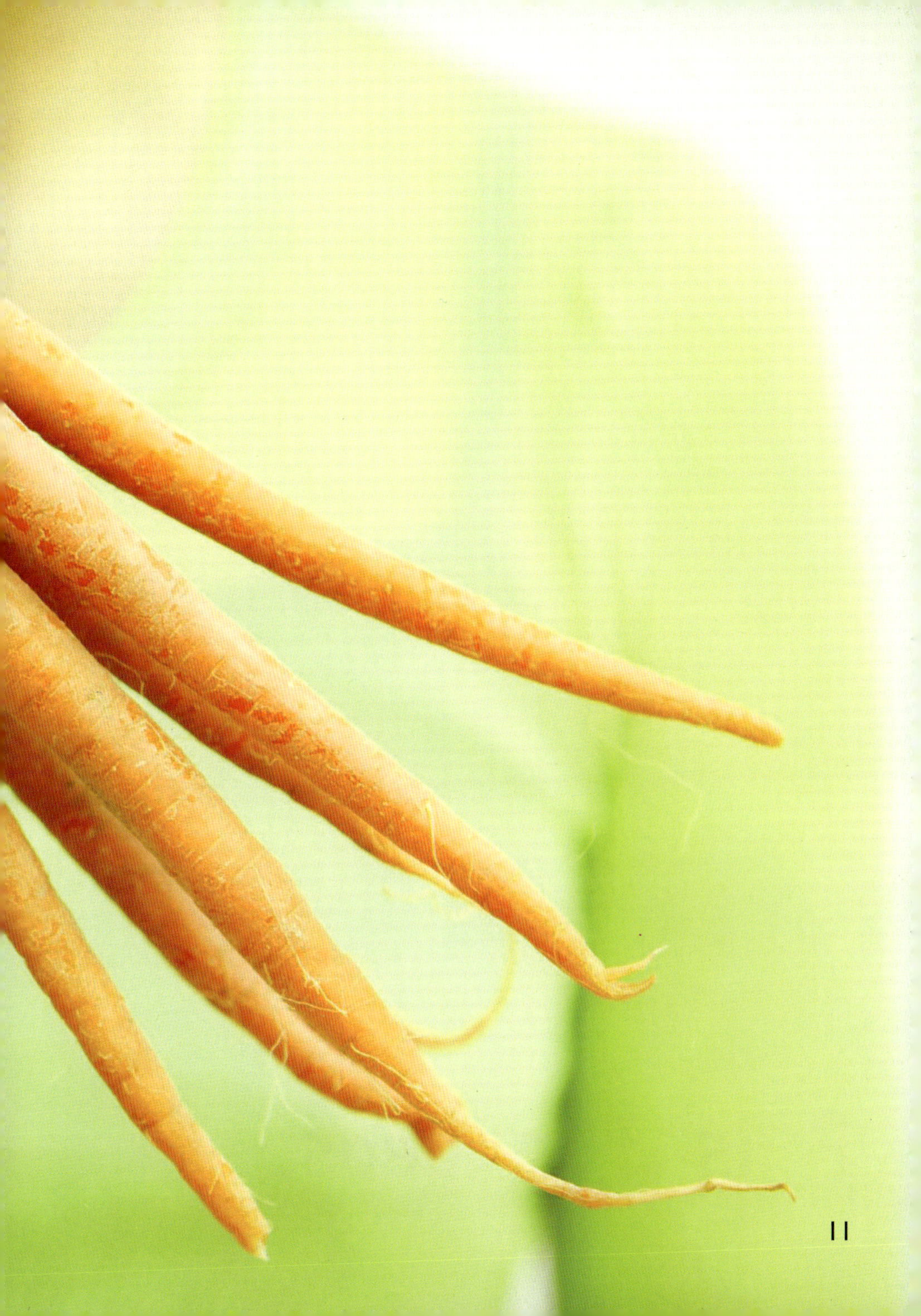

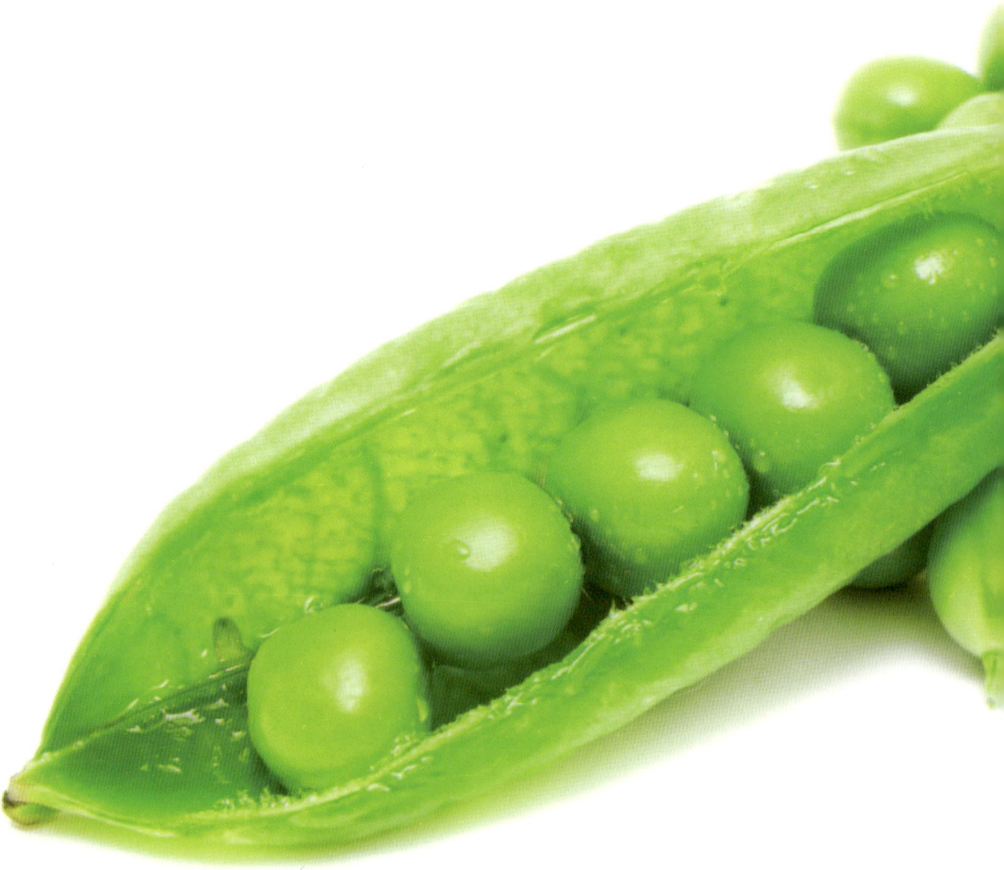

P is for peas.

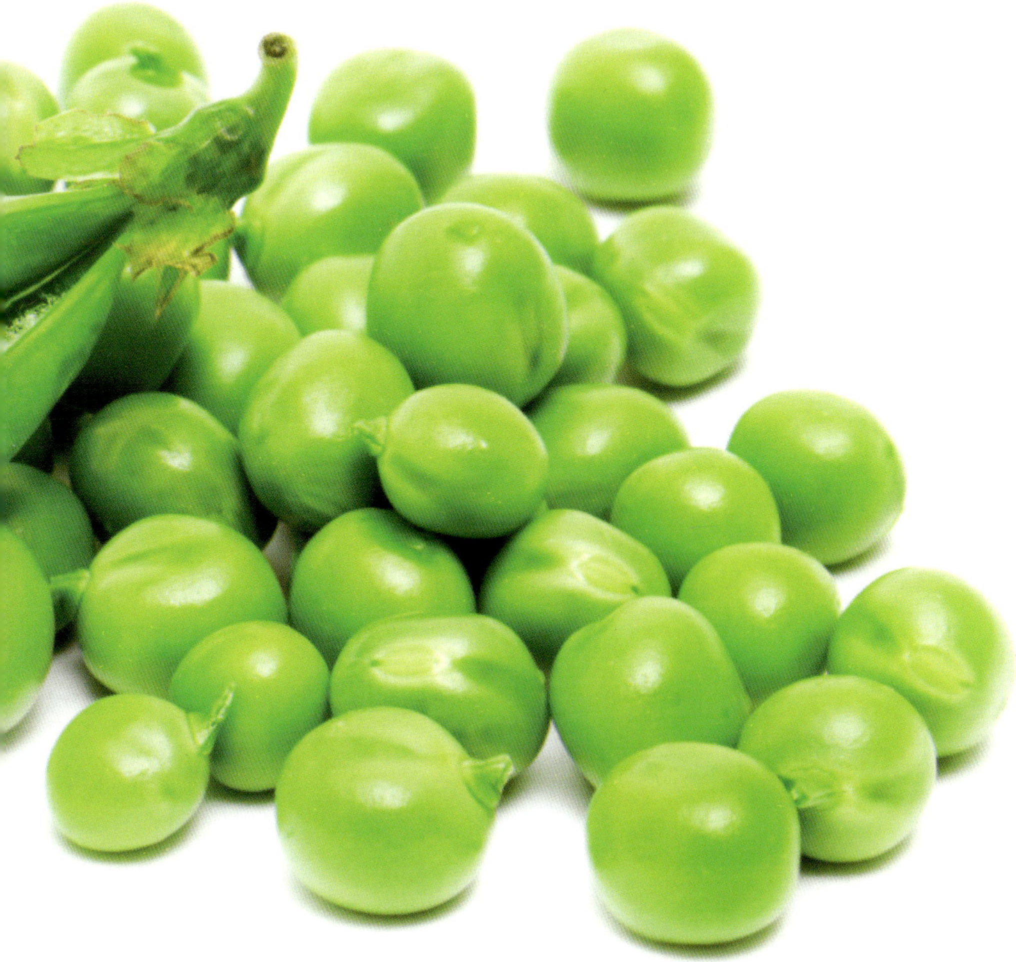

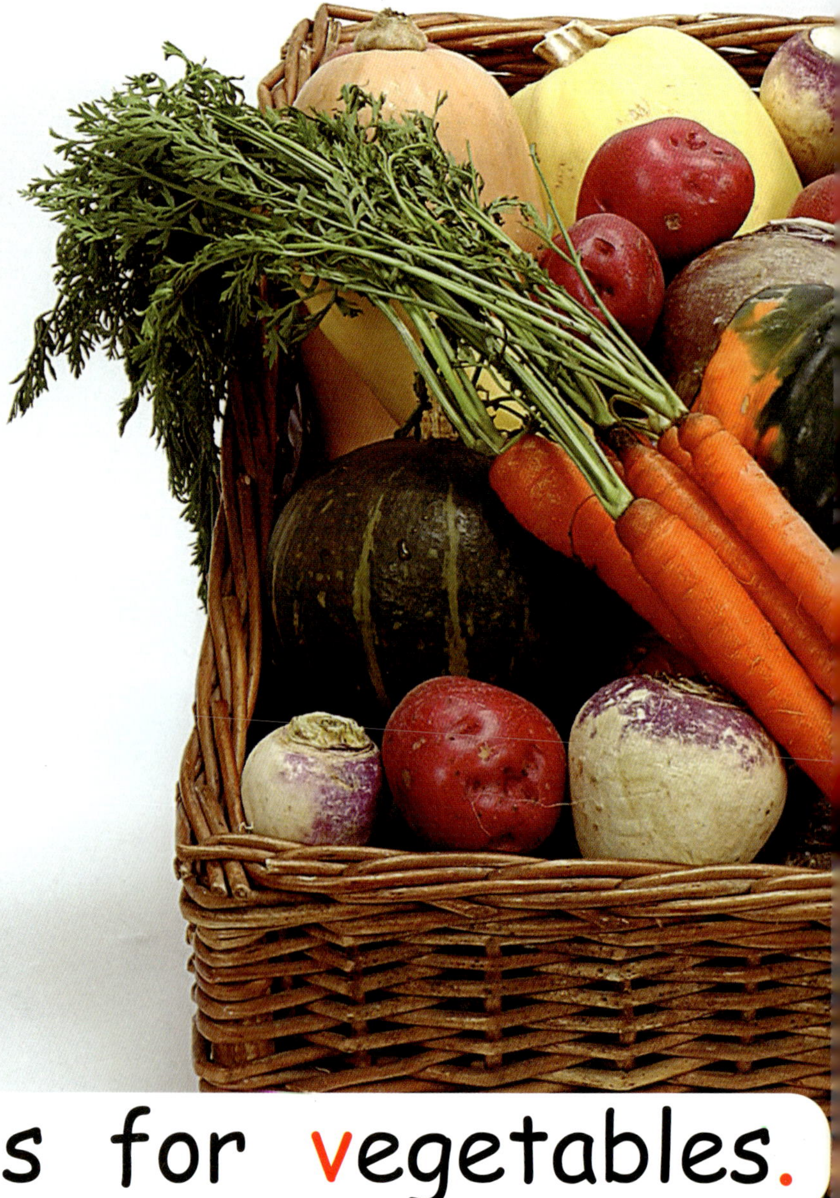

V is for vegetables.

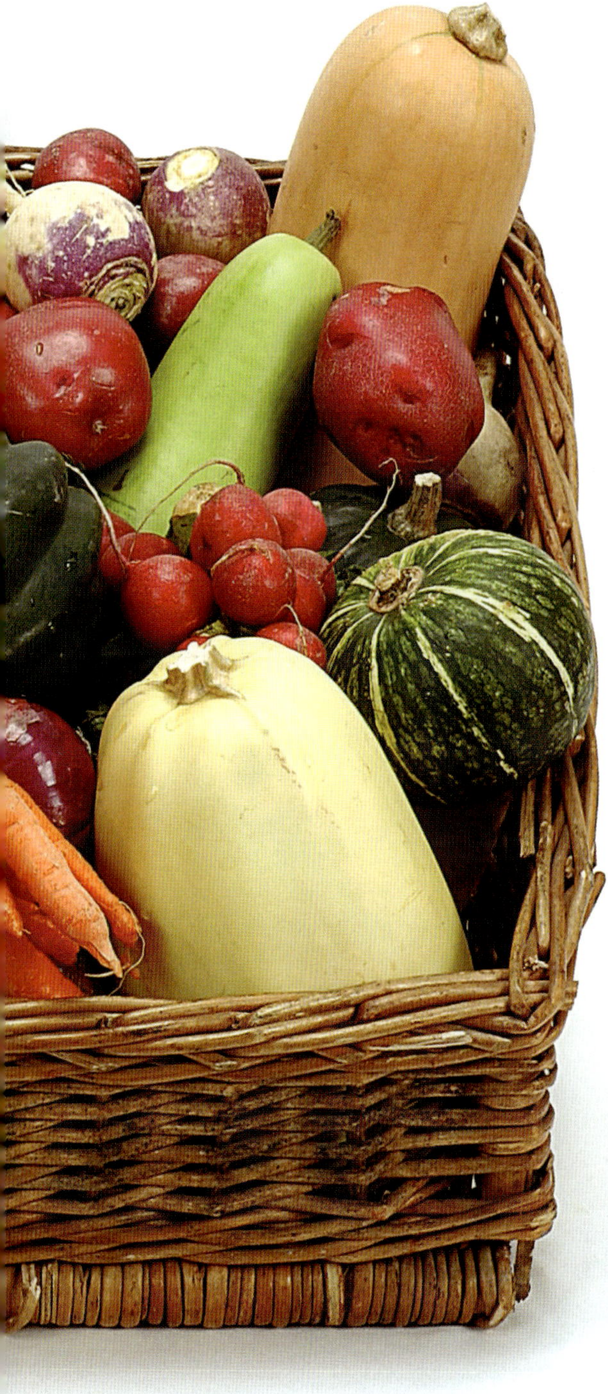

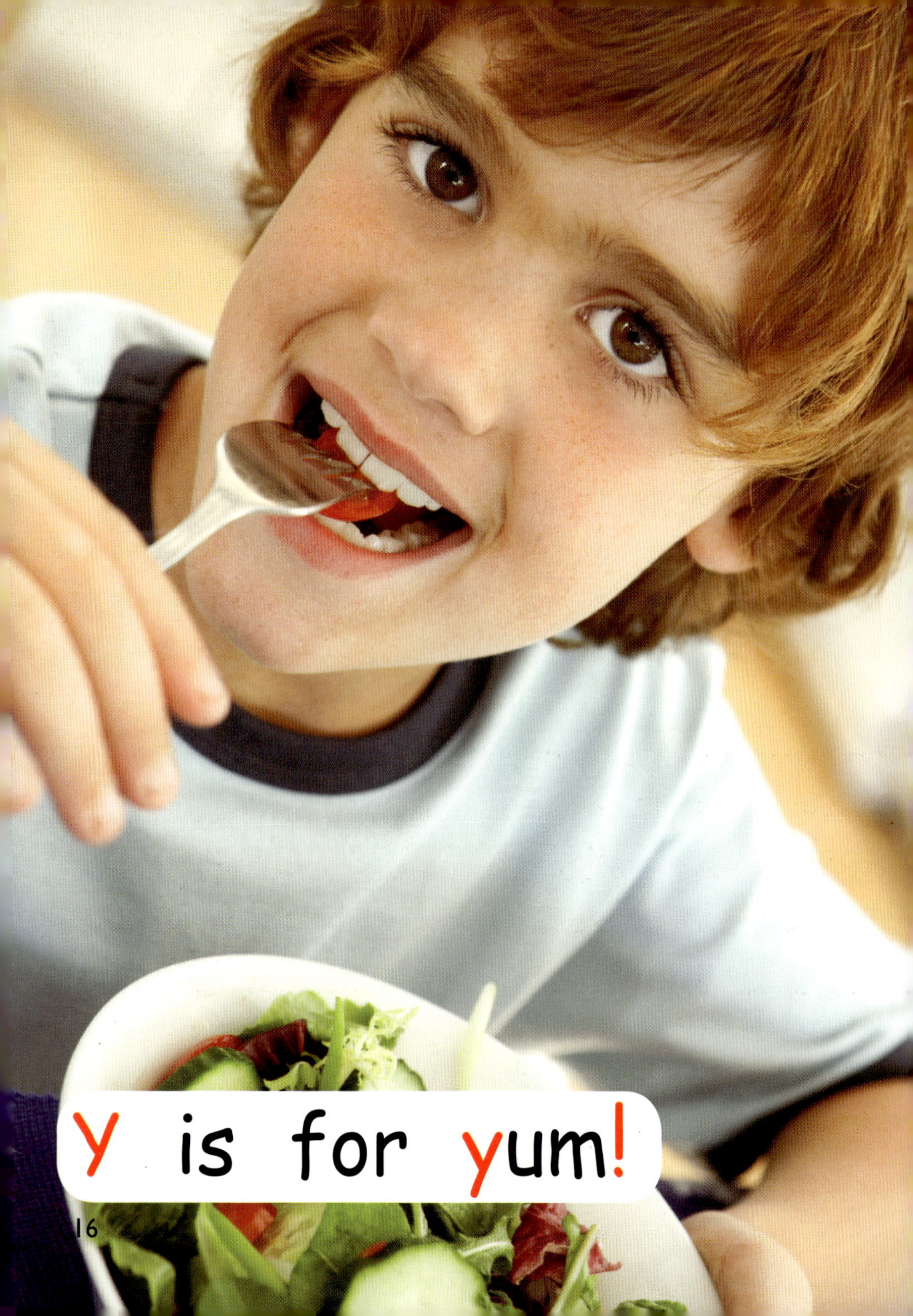

Y is for yum!